Super Bowl MVP Leads Title Defense in 2008

ELI MANNING

AND BIG BLUE

TRIUMPH
BOOKS

NEW YORK POST

MVP Eli Manning celebrates amidst a throng of journalists in the wake of victory in Super Bowl XLII.

Triumph Books and colophon are registered
trademarks of Random House, Inc.

This book is available in quantity at special discounts for your group
or organization. For further information, contact:

Triumph Books
542 South Dearborn Street
Suite 750
Chicago, Illinois 60605
(312) 939-3330
Fax (312) 663-3557

Printed in United States of America
ISBN: 978-1-60078-156-8

Photos courtesy of New York Post/Charles Wenzelberg except where otherwise noted.
Photo Editors: Joseph Amari and Evelyn Cordon

Content packaged by Mojo Media, Inc.
Joe Funk: Editor
Jason Hinman: Creative Director

Contents

Michael Strahan shows off the Vince Lombardi Trophy while riding a float during the Giants' victory parade.

By Mike Vaccaro

It's Why They Play the Game

The ball was in the air for what felt like a lifetime, and David Tyree was perfectly willing to wait it out that long if that's what it took. All around him, the Super Bowl had come to a complete standstill. All around him, every eye, thousands of them, were fastened on a football.

"I couldn't hear a thing," Tyree said. "I felt like I was all by myself."

There were, in reality, 71,101 spectators inside University of Phoenix Stadium. There were a couple-hundred others, give or take, patrolling the sideline: players, coaches, photographers, officials, various other folks with lanyards and credentials around their necks. All of them entranced by the football; all of them seized by the moment. Half of them had come in search of perfection, hoping for a rare glimpse of history, waiting for the New England Patriots to complete a 19–0 season, something that had never before been done in the NFL. Half of them had come bearing the thinnest sliver of belief that they would see an underdog rise out of the dust and the desert, a literal phoenix in Phoenix, the Giants attempting to usurp the throne. The Patriots had been professional assassins all season, relishing their role as America's Most Disliked Team. The Giants had settled nicely into the role of cuddly upstarts, with three road-playoff wins in the bank already, and arrived in Arizona bearing the look of gamblers with house money filling their pockets.

"Nobody expects us to do anything," Michael Strahan, the Hall of Fame–bound defensive lineman, had crowed earlier in the week. "If we lose, we're not doing anything but what the people expect. And if we win…hell, if you keep score, anything can happen."

He let the thought linger out there, because it was too fantastic to ponder. But Strahan believed. All of them did. Some even took the unexpected step of saying so on the record. Giants fans winced. Patriots fans pounced. The

The famous catch: David Tyree pins the ball to his helmet, hanging on and creating one of the most enduring images of Super Bowl XLII.

usual chatter of Super Bowl week ensued. And then, in a heartbeat, it was all prologue. None of it mattered, not with fewer than two minutes remaining in the football season, with the Patriots leading 14–10 and looking to lay a hammer down on the Giants' skulls once and for all, once and forever. This mattered: Eli Manning, a half-second away from absorbing a crunching sandwich of a sack, dancing a Gene Kelly two-step out of harm's way. A football in the air. A Super Bowl at a standstill. Two seasons, two destinies, one championship literally up in the air.

The air was thick with desperation, with the unmistakable whiff of imminent crisis. Outside was a muggy and suffocating late September in Washington, D.C., which turned FedEx Field into a humid quagmire. Inside, in the visitors' locker room, was something else.

"Guys," Tom Coughlin announced, "This is the time for us to find out who we are as a team. It's as simple as that."

In the past, this message may have been delivered at a higher decibel level, with a shade of sarcasm frosting the words, with quivering anger audible in every syllable. The Giants already were 0–2. They already were trailing the Redskins 17–3, staring at the abyss. Every now and again, a team finds a way to recover from 0–3. More often what you get is a one-way ticket to disaster. But Coughlin had promised things would be different this year.

In this uncomfortable moment, the Giants could have dismissed him. But he proved to be a man of his word. In Albany, training camp had seemed less like Parris Island. There had been a famous bowling night out. There was a freshly formed leadership council that already had solidified the bonds between staff and roster. What followed was the first dividend.

"Fellas," Strahan announced, "We're going to win this game."

Strahan had long been an unquestioned locker-room leader, 15 years of excellence earning him that place of prominence. That wasn't always a good thing. Strahan's moods occasionally turned dark and sour, clouding the room. He and Coughlin had a rough start, the player used to one set of standards, the coach demanding another. Yet it was Strahan who'd made the first move simply by deciding not to retire. His teammates voted him captain, though he never set foot in Albany for that training camp. In the past, that probably would have been impossible for Coughlin to stomach. Not anymore. He needed allies.

"The season starts right here," Strahan said, "Right now."

The new season began with the Giants reeling off 21 unanswered points, then heroically keeping the Redskins out of the end zone in the final minute, stoning them four straight times. Six straight wins followed. Suddenly, in a weak conference, the Giants were solid contenders. Most days, Giants fans could even allow themselves the occasional leap of faith, believing they had the

Plaxico Burress hauled in this Manning pass for the decisive score in Super Bowl XLII.

Four weeks later, inside the swirling, snowy bowl of Ralph Wilson Stadium, he may have been even worse, fumbling the ball five times, throwing two picks, and allowing the pedestrian Bills to haunt and spook him. He ultimately had to rely on two long touchdown runs by Brandon Jacobs and Ahmad Bradshaw (quietly emerging as precisely the kind of one-two running punch the Giants needed to allow Eli to manage games rather than dominate them) and a terrific effort by the Giants' defense. It should have been a feel-good day, two days before Christmas. The Giants thrashed Buffalo, 38–21, and wrapped up a playoff spot. And later in the day, when the Redskins went into Minnesota and beat the Vikings, it all but assured that the Giants would gain a favorable playoff slot, drawing the Buccaneers in Tampa rather than the Seahawks in Seattle. But really, it didn't seem to matter whom they played or where they played. Not as long as their quarterback was this bad.

necessary ingredients to piece together a playoff run. There was only one problem with that formula: the quarterback kept getting in the way.

It was hard to determine where the low point came. Week 12 was a good place to start, when Minnesota visited the Meadowlands and threw a frightening jolt of uneasiness into the whole of Giants Nation and the hole of the Giants offense. Eli Manning threw four interceptions that day. Three were returned for Vikings touchdowns, and the final score was 41–17. The repercussions were resounding.

"It's pretty simple," Coughlin said. "We need the quarterback to play better than that. He knows it. He's not trying to throw interceptions. He's playing hard. He just needs to be better."

"I still have confidence," Eli said, but he said it in the monotonic voice that had started to drive New York City crazy, his room-temperature outlook starting to look like a bad fit for the city's high-octane perspectives. "I know what I'm capable of doing. I know that I can be a

For all of their boasting about 19-0, the Patriots ended up falling short. Giants fans were quick to pounce on the opportunity to rub in their victory.

good quarterback in this league. And I will be a good quarterback."

New York nodded, and listened, and wanted to believe. A week later, Manning looked sharp against the Patriots, a game less notable for that than for the fact that Coughlin decided to play his regulars, and play them all game long, despite the fact that there was nothing tangible to be gained. The Giants were a locked-in five-seed in the playoffs.

"The question is a little frustrating, to be honest with you," the coach said. "The Patriots are 15–0, and they'll be playing to win the game. Why shouldn't we?"

Again, there was another concession from the new Coughlin, the open-minded Coughlin. His

players badly wanted to play the game. They wanted a crack at the Pats, because it was so unlikely they would ever get another one. He decided to let them play for a half. Then for three quarters. And then the whole game. The Pats won, 38–35. But it hardly felt like a loss for the Giants.

"We know how good we can be," Amani Toomer said afterward. "If we didn't, we just showed it all over again. You can't have a 12-point lead on a team that good if you aren't pretty good yourself."

They were pretty good. But pretty good and playoffs don't often go together.

Except, as it turned out, they were a bit better than pretty good. In Tampa, in the 80-degree heat, they wore down the Buccaneers and won the franchise's first playoff game in seven years, 24–14. In Dallas, with the glitter twins of Tony Romo and Terrell Owens waiting for them, they ground down the Cowboys, reducing Texas Stadium to a whisper with a 21–17 win. Quietly, the quarterback had played a second straight terrific game, outplaying Romo the way he'd outplayed erstwhile Giant-killer Jeff Garcia the week before.

"He's the best quarterback I've ever played with," Jacobs gushed. "You can have anyone else you want. I want Eli."

That vast field of candidates would include Brett Favre, waiting for Eli and the Giants in the subzero frost of Green Bay a week later. There was no way the Giants were walking into Lambeau Field and doing battle with both the

Patriots coach Bill Belichick may be one of the finest minds in the NFL, but scandal hounded him and his team all season.

14–3 Packers and the ghost of Lombardi and walking away with the George Halas Trophy. That was clear. Vegas almost laughed when it posted a seven-point spread. That seemed kind.

"We like Vegas," linebacker Antonio Pierce said, smiling. "They're like everybody else, underestimating us. I like that. It gives us fuel."

They needed that fuel at Lambeau, where the temperature dipped to minus-four degrees with a windchill of 23 below, where just breathing was an adventure, and where Lawrence Tynes, the Scottish-born kicker, made it even more audacious by missing two fourth-quarter field goals to keep the Packers alive. The game went to overtime. Old Giants fans still have very queasy memories of playoff overtimes. Some remember Flipper Anderson. Many more remember Alan Ameche. This time, they would remember Favre, throwing an inexplicable ball that Corey Webster picked off. And they would remember every bit what they were feeling as they watched Tynes get a third chance at glory, booting a football through the chill of Lambeau…the Giants' season literally up in the air, and not for the last time.

The fact that the ball was in the air at all was a miracle, of course. Eli Manning is good at many things, but escaping is not one of them. Yet he had gotten free and heaved the ball. There was a time, maybe as recently as two months earlier, where a heaved Eli Manning ball meant one thing: an easy interception, which in this case would have meant a season-ending interception.

Tyree and Rodney Harrison were both poised, looking at the ball, like two kids playing catchers-flies-up. Both went for the ball. Both jumped. Tyree's hands hit leather first, and he trapped the ball against his helmet, of all things. He then reached around, held on tight, and waited for impact. An Immaculate Connection. And there, in one snapshot, you have your 2007 New York Giants, your *Super Bowl XLII champion* New York Giants. You have a ball in the air and a championship in the balance, and no one—no one—believing that David Tyree would beat the great Rodney Harrison to that ball. And yet he beat him anyway.

A few moments later, Manning found Plaxico Burress in the end zone, and a few minutes after that Tom Brady's fourth-down prayer found the grass, and a few minutes after that Eli Manning's knee found the turf, and then the final gun went off, and man, oh, man, people will be talking about all of that for as long as they play football games. Or any kind of sports, for that matter. Knowing that if they keep score, anything can happen. ∎

Manning embraces powerhouse running back Brandon Jacobs, one of the key contributors to the Giants' late-season offensive resurgence.

By Steve Serby

The Mann: MVP Eli Did it His Way

YOU thought you would never live long enough to see another Charley Conerly, or Y.A. Tittle, or Phil Simms. You spent most of the past four years wondering whether Eli Manning was actually related to Big Brother Peyton Manning, or even his dad, Archie Manning. You wished your Giants had drafted Ben Roethlisberger, or kept Philip Rivers.

And then, without warning, when it mattered most, with Tony Romo, Brett Favre, and Tom Brady and the perfect Patriots standing in his way, the boy wearing No. 10 became a Mann. A SuperMann. YOUR SuperMann.

You underestimated him. We all did. He wasn't a leader. His body language made you think he was a milquetoast mope. He wasn't accurate enough. From the time he took over midway through his rookie season for Kurt Warner, he was up and down. He was Eli Maddening. He couldn't win a playoff game. He was so quiet, so private, so far removed from being a Broadway Joe, that you

feared he was the wrong quarterback, the wrong Mann, for New York.

Look at him now. Look at him, right up there on that Big Blue pedestal where only Conerly, Tittle, and Simms stand forever. Our latest, greatest Comeback Kid. Joe Namath won one championship, the AFL Jets' immortal Super Bowl III upset of the NFL Baltimore Colts. Eli Manning just tied him, with an immortal shock-the-world triumph of his own. "I never doubted myself," Eli said the morning after Super Bowl XLII. "I never lost confidence . . . I'm very comfortable in my own skin. I am the way I am, and I wasn't going to change."

And look at you now, euphoric that you have finally found your long-lost franchise quarterback, your Hope diamond, just 27 years old, and damn well capable of bringing another championship home, and soon.

He fooled you. He fooled us all. Perhaps we should have suspected that he was made of the

After four years of doubt and speculation from fans, Eli Manning finally came into his own and showed his championship mettle.

Manning locks onto Plaxico Burress streaking over the middle.

right stuff the way his teammates never stopped believing in him. Through thick and thin, they saw what football, what winning, meant to him. The mask he wears all the time hid that quiet fire that rages inside him. Big Brother finally winning his Super Bowl last year only fueled that quiet fire.

It turns out he was born for that profile-in-courage moment, that last-minute drive in the fourth quarter when the Giants and New York asked him to please get them that Lombardi Trophy.

"If he is what we thought he was," former Giants GM Ernie Accorsi, who brought Manning to New York with that draft-day blockbuster trade, thought to himself, "he's gotta do it now." It was that very cool, calm, collected temperament that so often made you gnash your teeth that saved him, and them, and you. Easy—such a fitting nickname —does it. It served him well, following his legendary father at Ole Miss, and now here.

He is the same calm guy every day, the way Derek Jeter is. Jeter has four rings. Eli's comin.'

"I'm a Super Bowl champion," Eli said. "I'm fired up and I'm going to enjoy this moment. You still want to do it again. You still want to have this feeling again." Mann for all seasons, and ages. ■

(above) While Tom Brady was easily the most celebrated quarterback in the NFL during the regular season, Manning would trump him in the game that mattered most. (opposite) Even diehard Giants fans still had their doubts about Manning, until he delivered a Super Bowl MVP performance.

By Mike Vaccaro

Eli Manning: The Early Years

All around him, the world had turned blurry with excitement, loud with anticipation. There were two minutes and 39 seconds remaining in this football game, the biggest football game of Eli Manning's life. All around him, people with microphones and with trophies were eager to coronate the other quarterback in the house, the other team on the field.

Tom Brady was about to lead the New England Patriots to their fourth Super Bowl title in seven years. The Patriots were two minutes and 39 seconds away from finishing off a perfect 19–0 season. All they had to do was stop Eli Manning and the New York Giants short of their own goal line, which stood 83 yards away.

There were 71,101 people inside University of Phoenix Stadium this third day of February, 2008, and they were at war with each other, with themselves, with their emotions, with their voice boxes. For much of the afternoon and evening of Super Bowl XLII, the Giants had allowed half of them to dream, half of them to fret; they'd been feisty and fearless and had even taken a 10–7 lead on the mighty Patriots in the fourth quarter.

But then Brady had found Randy Moss in the end zone, the Patriots had sneaked back into a 14–10 lead, and now they weren't only pursuing the Giants at University of Phoenix Stadium, but into history. The Pats knew what they needed to do.

"We need to get the quarterback!" defensive lineman Richard Seymour yelled over the din.

"Crush him and we crush them!" screeched safety Rodney Harrison.

A few yards away, in the Giants huddle, things were calmer. Much calmer. For the first few years of his career, Eli Manning had been a passive enigma in his own huddle, often the third or fourth most-prominent voice heard. Not now. Not anymore. Not with two minutes and 39 seconds left in this magnificent game, with 83 yards separating the Giants and unimaginable glory.

Following in the footsteps of dad Archie, Eli Manning honed his craft and became a top prospect while quarterbacking at Ole Miss.

Now, this was his huddle. His office.

"Let's go win this thing," Eli Manning said. "Who's with me?"

* * *

Other kids would have grown up bathed in resentment, weighed down hard with the burdens and the baggage of the Name.

There was never any escaping it for Eli Manning, not from the moment he arrived in the world on January 3, 1981, in New Orleans. His father, Archie, was already a 10-year professional quarterback, having served nobly, if painfully, in the service of the hometown Saints. He'd already secured a slice of football immortality at Ole Miss, where he'd not only thrown for 4,753 yards and 56 touchdowns as a three-year starter, but also met and married Olivia, Eli's mother.

Soon enough, Eli would morph from being the Son to the Brother. First, his oldest sibling, Cooper, became a star receiver at Isidore Newman School (and a recruit to Ole Miss, before having to quit football due to a spinal injury). Later, Peyton, the middle brother, grew into the most celebrated prep quarterback in the nation at Newman and an All-America quarterback at Tennessee. Peyton went on to become

(above) Posing with Archie and Peyton at the NFL Draft, Eli Manning is the third member of his family to be a pro passer. (opposite) By the time his college career was in full swing, Manning had gone from being Archie's Son to Peyton's Brother.

the No. 1 pick in the 1998 NFL Draft and one of the greatest quarterbacks in the league's history, capped by an MVP performance during the Indianapolis Colts' 29–17 win over the Chicago Bears in Super Bowl XLI.

It was in the aftermath of that day—the most triumphant day in the Manning family's football history—that Olivia Manning had said something that was either roundly ignored (at best), chuckled over (at least), or mocked (at worst) as the warblings of a proud mother.

"Maybe next year," she said, "it can be Eli's turn."

At that precise moment, Eli, the youngest Manning, was approaching a serious crossroads in his quarterbacking life. Eli had been just as ballyhooed as his brother coming out of Newman (both completed 59 percent of their passes in their respective senior years) and had gone to Ole Miss and had a splendid career—10,119 yards and 81 touchdowns—dwarfing his father's numbers there.

In a game during his junior year against Auburn, Ernie Accorsi, the general manager of the Giants, had watched him riddle the Tigers' superior defense and singlehandedly keep the Rebels in a game they wound up losing. Accorsi, who in a previous life as GM of the Colts had drafted John Elway, and who counted among his closest friends the late Johnny Unitas, was smitten. He was retiring soon. He saw in Eli Manning one last chance to draft a franchise quarterback. And on draft day 2004, he moved heaven and earth to get him, swapping Philip Rivers and two other No. 1 picks to San Diego.

"If it was easy to become a great NFL quarterback, then more guys would do it, and we wouldn't rhapsodize so much about Unitas, or Dan Marino, or Joe Montana, or Tom Brady," Accorsi would say a few years later. "But it isn't easy. It's hard. It may be the hardest job in sports. You need so much: brains, a strong arm, nimble feet, toughness. It helps to be unflappable. But you're going to take your lumps, take your hits. You're going to suffer a lot before you enjoy the benefits. *If* you enjoy the benefits."

By December 2007, Eli Manning was still mostly waiting for the benefits. He'd been given the starting job midway through his rookie season, replacing the aging Kurt Warner. In 2005, he'd shown signs of an early breakthrough, led the Giants to the NFC East championship, but flamed out badly in a playoff loss to Carolina. Then, after the Giants started the next season 6–2, Manning was one of the chief engineers of a collapse that nearly swallowed the Giants whole and cost coach Tom Coughlin his job, a 2–7 freefall that included a playoff loss in Philadelphia to the Eagles.

Nothing was certain about Eli Manning anymore. Just before the start of the 2007 season, Tiki Barber, once Manning's chief offensive weapon but now a full-time television commentator, delivered this stinging appraisal of Manning's qualities as a leader: "His personality hasn't been so that he can step up, make a strong statement, and have people

Despite flashes of brilliance earlier in his career, fans didn't know what to expect from Manning going into 2007.

believe that it's coming from his heart. He didn't feel like his voice was going to be strong enough, and it showed. Sometimes it was almost comical the way that he would say things."

Manning's reponse—"I guess I'm just happy for Tiki that he's making a smooth transition into the TV world"—was either an example of Accorsi's "unflappable" characterization or a reinforcement of everything Barber had just said, depending on how you looked at it.

And by December, it was hard to look at it any other way. Manning had been very good in stretches. But then, in November, he'd thrown four interceptions against the Minnesota Vikings, three of which were returned for touchdowns. In December, in Buffalo, in a game the Giants needed to win to clinch a playoff berth, he'd been so bad that Coughlin all but designed a second-half game plan that tried to keep Manning's hands off the ball as much as possible after he threw two more picks and fumbled the ball five times (losing two).

"I have to be better than that," a glum Manning admitted.

"Obviously, we need him to be better than that," a worried Coughlin conceded.

Coughlin and others started using the frightening euphemism "game manager" when referring to Eli now. No one ever called Montana a "game manager," or Marino, or even Joe Namath, who was known to commit a turnover or three. The Giants, by general consensus, were going

nowhere unless the quarterback stopped being a liability and started playing like a weapon.

And then a funny thing happened.

In the playoff opener, against the Buccaneers in Tampa Bay, he completed 20 out of 27 passes for 185 yards, two touchdowns, and zero interceptions.

The next week, against the Cowboys in Texas, he was 12 for 18 and had 163 yards, two touchdowns, and zero interceptions.

And the next week, in the subzero conditions of Green Bay's Lambeau Field, he was 21 for 40, had 251 yards, no touchdowns but, again, zero interceptions. And he was on the sideline in overtime when Brett Favre, the sainted, swashbuckling quarterback who was everything Eli was not in every way, threw the key pick that led to the field goal that landed the Giants in the Super Bowl. Landed Eli Manning in the Super Bowl.

"I don't think the bad things that were said about him ever affected him, because he's just not that way," Archie said outside the Giants' locker room that evening. "And look, I never thought he was ever as bad as he was made out to be. And so I'm not going to stand here and tell you he's ready to move Phil Simms out of the books, either. But he's a young quarterback getting better all the time."

Sixty minutes away from something only his mother could have dreamed of.

* * *

And now it was less than three minutes. Two minutes and 39 seconds, to be precise.

In the harsh conditions of Lambeau Field, it was the legendary Brett Favre who made the crucial mistake: the final pass of his career went for the interception that led to the field goal that sent the Giants to the Super Bowl.

"Let's go win this thing," Eli Manning said. "Who's with me?"

"That's what I'm here for," Plaxico Burress, his favorite receiver said.

"Let's go 80 yards," David Diehl, one of his linemen, said.

This was his office now. His huddle. So he could edit his teammates now.

"Eighty-three yards is better," Eli said.

To that point, he had thrown 25 passes, completed 14, thrown a touchdown, and had one hard-luck interception, his first of the play-offs. Now, he started with a short 11-yard toss to Amani Toomer, then two incompletions before the two-minute warning, followed by a nine-yarder to Toomer.

Staring at fourth-and-one, Brandon Jacobs bulled for two.

"You're a man!" Eli yelled at the running back, back in his office. There was 1:34 left. He scrambled for five, threw a deep incompletion in the general direction of David Tyree. Third-and-five, 1:20 left.

And then it happened.

Every superb athlete has a signature moment, one immortalized by capital letters. Willie Mays had the Catch. Elway had the Drive. Franco Harris had the Immaculate Reception. Now, as Eli danced out of trouble, as he eluded a certain sack, and then did it again, and then flung the ball down-field, he was about to have himself a moment.

The Moment.

Tyree jumped, came down, trapped the ball against his helmet, and fell on Harrison. And held on to the ball. Thirty-two yards in all. First and 10 at the Patriots 24. Fifty-nine seconds left. Manning lost a yard on a sack. Threw incomplete toward Tyree again. Then found another kid receiver, Steve Smith, for 13 yards, down to the Patriots' 13.

Thirty-nine seconds left.

What was it that Manning had said exactly two minutes earlier? "Let's go win this thing." What was it that Burress had replied? "That's what I'm here for." And now, with bedlam breaking out around them, Manning dropped back, and Burress made a head fake, and the ball was in the air.

Touchdown. Giants 17, Patriots 14. The Pats tried to rally but could not. With one second left, the ball back in his hands, Eli Manning took one last snap, kneeled down, and that was it. The Son, the Brother, he was now his own man. He was a champion.

"I'm still me," he said.

And that, it turned out, was plenty. ▪

After taking a knee to end Super Bowl XLII, Manning and his teammates could now call themselves champions.

"I never tried to do anything different. I never tried to talk just so people would see me talking or scream or yell so somebody would see me do that. You got to do what you feel is right, if you're fake it will be obvious and the players will see that. You can't try to do something to please the media, but hurt your team."
—Eli Manning on the NY spotlight

"He's done an unbelievable job. He's had a lot of criticism himself. If I'm No. 1, he's No. 2 or vice versa, it's hard to say which is more. He had faith in me, I had faith in him, and this year he did a great job. He knew he had good veteran leaders on this team, and he let us lead the team, and he had faith that we could get it done." —*Eli Manning on his coach, Tom Coughlin*

"As a quarterback, I've had an appreciation for Eli's ability to remain calm in the highest pressure situations. The best quarterbacks are able to win in those moments as opposed to being overwhelmed by them."
—*Peyton Manning on Eli*

"I'm just as excited as every Giant fan in the country."
—*Proud papa Archie Manning after the Giants Super Bowl win*

"It's all 'What have you done for me lately?' As long as you keep winning you'll be fine. If something happens and you lose a game they'll be back on it. You can't try to be someone you're not, you can't try to act a certain way to please everybody. You got to be yourself. You got to do it the way you know."
—*Eli Manning on NY fans' doubts about him*

Q&A
with Tom Coughlin

The *Post*'s Steve Serby chatted with the Giants coach during his second preseason camp in 2005.

Q: Why weren't free agents scared away by Tom Coughlin?

A: They never are.

Q: There was a story with players grumbling anonymously about you last year in the *Post*. Is it okay to be hated?

A: As long as there's respect. Nobody wants to be hated. If they hated me last year, they should have seen me 10 years ago!

Q: What were you like back then?

A: In terms of goals, aspirations, principles and beliefs, I am the same person that I was then. If you are going to be the very best you can be, you're always looking for a better, more efficient way to achieve success. So I may have changed some of my methods, and I will always look to improve the method by which we operate.

Q: Where does Tom Coughlin have to get better?

A: I've got to continue to motivate and inspire our players to be the best they can be, and create, hopefully, an atmosphere where the players feel so good about their preparation that the challenge on Sunday is for them to allow their instinct and ability to take over. I'd like to see us in more game-winning circumstances and situations, and the more improved we are, the more that's going to happen. I'd like to be able to utilize some of our talent with greater imagination and detail.

Q: You have more playmakers this year?

A: On paper we do.

Q: Kareem McKenzie?

A: A big, powerful man who solidifies our offensive line.

Despite having to battle through some rough patches in his time in New York, Tom Coughlin has worked through the criticism to make his team better every time they step on the field.

"One thing I never doubted about him was his character and his work ethic and his belief in the fact that he could win a championship. I told him when we hired him that 'I wanted you as our coach since 1993 and we had to wait a long time to get you, and you know what, though? It was worth the wait.' "
—*Giants co-owner John Mara on Tom Coughlin*

Q: Antonio Pierce?

A: He works at the game. He studies football. He'll grab a young linebacker, take him in the room, and look at a tape with him. He's always challenging himself, never satisfied, always trying to get better.

Q: Plaxico Burress?

A: Big, fast, athletic, outstanding hands. A factor in the green zone, being up above everybody.

Q: Brandon Jacobs?

A: A big, powerful runner who has good hands. We have to be absolutely sure he becomes a good pass protector and gets you the yard if it's third-and-short, fourth-and-short.

Q: Shockey as more of a pass-catching threat?

A: We try to put Jeremy in a lot of different positions where it's most difficult to double him or figure out what he's going to do. All of those have in mind throwing the ball to him. He's also a good blocker, and his presence is felt on the line of scrimmage.

Q: How high is up for Eli Manning?

A: How high's the sky? He's humble and has outstanding interaction with his teammates. He wants to pay the price to be the best he can be.

Q: He probably thinks about football as much as you do.

A: I don't think there's any time during the day when he's not thinking about it.

Q: What about you?

A: Very rarely. If it's not [number] one, it's two. When my wife's around I'd have to say it's two (smiles).

Q: What words are beside "Tom Coughlin football player" in the dictionary?

A: Reliable, accountable, honest, dedicated, determined, mature, willing to pay the price to win or be the best he can be. Proud to wear the Giant blue. Takes ownership and responsibility for his job.

Q: Do you get hungrier to win a Super Bowl as you get older?

A: You do. That's what we're here for. I'm not here to be second.

Q: Why a full-team conditioning test at the start of training camp this year?

A: It allows us to make a statement, each individual to his teammates, about how well he's focused for the season.

Q: What if a player fails the test?

A: They will condition as we go along to where we think they're in the kind of shape they should be in.

Q: How many players take this game as seriously as you?

A: No player can be as serious as a coach. I want the player to be focused when he comes in that door. He doesn't have to carry it around 24 hours a day like a coach. His pride is 24 hours a day. His belief in being a part of his team is 24 hours a day. Winning in a competitive matter is 24 hours a day. But he has to be prepared to the point where he's instinctive, and then his love for the game and going and playing has to prevail.

Q: Did your first Giants team take the game seriously?

A: I was proud of the way the majority of our players hung in last year. That group that went out and won that last game [to break an eight-game losing streak and finish 6–10], they were pretty darn serious about what they were doing.

Q: Can this team make the kind of leap that your Jacksonville team made from year one [4–12] to year two [9–7]?

A: That team put together seven straight wins to just barely crawl into the playoffs. When players start to feel good about themselves, they have fun doing things which they called mundane and hard before. What I would like to see is them playing the best they can play, having fun doing it, looking forward to every challenge, and spreading the word among themselves.

Q: The best part about coaching in New York?

A: Being with this great franchise. Accepting the challenge we've accepted. Working with a bunch of young men with our eye on the restoration of New York Giant pride.

Q: The worst part of coaching in New York?

A: The anxiety, the frustration, the wanting to be good right now, this second.

Q: How often did you sleep in your office last year?

A: Once a week. Tuesday night. Game-plan night.

Q: Five greatest Americans?

A: Not in any order: George Washington, Abraham Lincoln, FDR, Dr. Martin Luther King, Eisenhower. All had the courage and vision to make a profound difference in the world.

Q: Best book you've read in the last year?

A: *Franklin and Winston* by Jon Meacham. It is about the relationship that Churchill and FDR had during the course of events of the second World War and how Churchill was so connected to FDR. ■

By Jay Greenberg

Tyree Grabs History and Holds on Tight

When David Tyree finally had a chance to witness what he had done, the guy who made what might have been the number one catch in Super Bowl history took a number amongst the incredulous.

"Until I saw it on TV with my own eyes, I didn't realize the magnitude of the catch and how great it was," he said.

With 1:15 left in Super Bowl XLII and the Giants trailing 14–10, up into the air at the Patriots' 24 rose Tyree for Eli Manning's third-and-five throw. Against the leap of All-Pro safety Rodney Harrison and against all odds, the Giants receiver trapped the 32-yard pass on the back of his helmet, then brought the ball around to his facemask while wresting control from Harrison and holding on through a jolting fall. For importance and degree of difficulty, there may never have been a more dramatic and spectacular reception. Four plays later, Eli Manning hit Plaxico Burress for a 13-yard touchdown pass to complete the 17–14 upset, one of the greatest in history. But it wasn't until many hours—and replays—later that it sunk in on the participants that this full-time special-teams ace and reserve receiver had pulled down a miracle.

"It's going to take me a good while to understand that it is going to be part of Super Bowl history," Tyree said. "For a guy like me, it's just an amazing feeling. I just knew I was at the high point, I had my hands on it, and I wasn't going to let go. I didn't know it was on the helmet, didn't know Rodney was ripping it out. I probably have one of the worst vertical leaps on the team. So the Lord put some bootsies in my jump to get up there."

Somebody had to be looking out for a guy who had lost his mother, Thelma, to a heart attack on December 15, 2007, and who wears his faith on his sleeve like a football on his helmet. Tyree had caught Manning's 15-yard touchdown pass to put the Giants ahead 10–7 3:50 into the fourth quarter, and yet still would have seemed

David Tyree jokingly recreates his famous catch, where he pinned the ball to his helmet in Super Bowl XLII and paved the way for the Giants' monumental upset.

With Rodney Harrison draped all over him,
Tyree hauls in what may go down as the most
famous catch in Giants history.

one of the least destined players on a team of destiny to rise so spectacularly.

"It's funny because I think he dropped almost every ball in practice Friday," Amani Toomer said. But GM Jerry Reese found Tyree the most appropriate hero fate could have chosen. "All he does is say, 'Coach, what do you want me to do?' He plays special teams, and when we needed him to make a tough catch in the middle, he does that too. That's what we're about. Usually at a Super Bowl, somebody comes out of the shadows, and it was David Tyree for us. You win championships with guys like that."

And enjoy them over and over again, too, watching their signature plays. Manning, who had almost as spectacularly eluded Jarvis Green and the jersey-clinging Richard Seymour before the fateful heave, was told by his brother Peyton Manning afterward that it was one of the greatest catches ever.

"Something we will remember forever," Tom Coughlin said. And Monday morning, Tyree was beginning to understand that there may not be a day the rest of his life when he will be allowed to forget.

"Am I ready for that?" he laughed. "I don't think I'm going to have much choice in the matter." ■

(above) GM Jerry Reese had always been impressed with Tyree's willingness to do whatever the team needed, and wasn't surprised that Tyree stepped up to make a crucial play when his team needed it. (opposite) Tyree's special teams prowess makes him a valuable member of the team in more ways than one.

AP Images

Q&A
with Chris Snee

The *Post*'s Steve Serby chatted with the Giants' right guard in 2008. His wife, Katie, is Tom Coughlin's daughter.

Q: The first time you met your father-in-law?

A: In the spring of sophomore year in college, he came up to BC to do one of those pro days—I think Will Green and Marc Colombo were the names coming out. He came up to watch them, and I went out to eat with Katie and Coach. I was pretty quiet, didn't say much…just answered the questions that were given to me…I was a little intimidated.

Q: Describe Thanksgiving Day with your father-in-law?

A: Well it starts with meetings and practice; I'm out of here much earlier than he is…I get [to dinner] around three, and he gets there at like six, 6:30.

Q: Does he carve the turkey?

A: Yeah.

Q: How good is he at that?

A: I don't know, I'm usually downstairs with the kids [sons Dylan and Cooper Christopher] or watching the game. I know his wife does a good job; she cooks it up good.

Q: Describe your mother-in-law [Judy].

A: She's a great woman. She's very easy to talk to…you can tell she's a great mother and also a great grandmother.

Q: Were you concerned about the nepotism thing when you were drafted?

A: I wasn't really worried about it, and to be honest with you, it wasn't bad at all.

Q: Dylan turned four in September…

A: He's just starting to understand kinda what I do; that makes it more enjoyable for me.

For Chris Snee, every day on the field means working with his father-in-law, Tom Coughlin.

Snee prides himself on playing with a mean
streak, but he's a family man off the field.

Q: Did you change diapers?

A: I did, I did. The potent ones I wasn't really good at changing for a while (smiles).

Q: Best practical joke Eli Manning has played recently?

A: It's tough to get a nab on him because he always denies that it's him, and I think the quarterbacks work together, all three of those guys, and even, I think [Chris] Palmer, the quarterback coach, is getting involved, too. Anyway it's quarterbacks against O-linemen.

Q: What did Eli pull on you in training camp?

A: I was in his room—I thought he wasn't there. I was kinda messing around his room a little bit. He opened up a couple cans of soda, shook 'em, sprayed 'em all over me, and then got me with that Silly String, which is a pain in the [neck] to get off.

Q: Best trash-talking defender?

A: [Last Saturday] it was obvious that Rodney Harrison won't shut his mouth…just keeps talking, looks for the cheap shot at the end.

Q: Did that tick you off?

A: A little bit, yeah.

Q: What'd you do about it?

A: Well we got into a little scuffle afterward, so…

Q: Your mentality on the field?

A: You have to play with a chip on your shoulder, play with a mean streak.

Q: You like inflicting punishment?

A: If you come out of a game and your body feels good, then obviously you weren't out there banging as much as you should have been.

Q: The "No Mercy" tattoo on your left arm?

A: I play with an edge on the field.

Q: Who is that figure beneath No Mercy.

A: This is the Grim Reaper.

Q: Most embarrassing moment?

A: [Center Shaun] O'Hara's the king of falling, but we all take our falls where you just look completely unathletic.

Q: Kareem McKenzie?

A: His new name is the Big Bear; he probably sleeps 20 hours a day, including his time here.

Q: Rich Seubert?

A: Seubert is known as the Grumpy Old Troll. He looks like a miserable, miserable human being, hobbles around here all day. On the field, he's feisty. He likes to scrap and fight and you'll see him many times after the whistle getting into something.

Q: O'Hara off the field?

A: He's a fun guy to be around…. He can carry a conversation—longer than you probably want (smiles).

Q: How did you propose to Katie?

A: We went out to eat in Boston, and we were just in a restaurant, and I had [the ring] in my pocket the whole time. I was a little nervous, wasn't sure when the right time was, and after dinner, I hit a knee and asked her. Initially, she said, "What are you doing?"

Q: Best Boston College moment?

A: I have two. One was obviously beating Notre Dame at their place. And the second one would have been when we went to Penn State; that was my favorite team growing up.

Q: How disappointed were you about not getting an offer from Penn State?

A: I grew up watching that Penn State football story every Sunday morning on whatever channel it was. Would have loved to go there, but obviously I wouldn't change anything.

Q: Describe Montrose, Pennsylvania.

A: One stoplight—does that do enough for you? (Smiles). My parents live on a dirt road...small town, everyone knows everybody. We had 21 guys on our high school team, so obviously you never came off the field.

Q: Favorite childhood memory?

A: The pickup football games I would play with my little brother and his friends. They were all bigger than me. We would do that every Saturday and Sunday. I was too heavy to play in any organized football.

Q: Did it bother you that you were too heavy to play at that point?

A: I thought, "Do I want to go on a diet, or do I just eat what I want?" I was having fun doing what I was doing, and I knew that I would play eventually.

Q: Were you a big eater?

A: I was a short, chubby, little kid. Seventh grade, I was 5' 2", 170 pounds, so I didn't grow until ninth grade, and I didn't look as chubby—some people might argue.

Q: 5' 2", 170?

A: I was a little bowling ball, man.

Q: Any nicknames?

A: My older brother used to call me everything— Fat Boy, Short Round.

Q: Boyhood idol?

A: My parents [Diane and Ed].

Q: Favorite movie?

A: *A Few Good Men.*

Q: Favorite actor?

A: Will Smith; De Niro.

Q: Favorite actress?

A: Demi Moore.

Q: Favorite entertainer?

A: Jerry Seinfeld.

Q: Favorite meal?

A: Spaghetti with meatballs.

By Paul Schwartz

Jints Make Sure Spags Stays

If there is any public office open in the New York/New Jersey area, Steve Spagnuolo could run and win in a heartbeat. At the moment, is there anyone more popular around here?

Already a rising star for his work as a first-year defensive coordinator, Spagnuolo made a meteoric ascension as the Giants rolled to one playoff win after another. Then, confronted with the impossible challenge of containing the most prolific offense in NFL history, Spagnuolo's unit not only kept the Giants within striking distance of the Patriots in Super Bowl XLII, but his defense pulverized Tom Brady and with a devastating show of force ground down the New England attack, paving the way for Eli Manning's final drive and a 17–14 upset for the ages. If Spagnuolo, who signed a three-year deal worth slightly more than $6 million, was adored by Giants fans after that astonishing performance, he became an absolute hero after turning down the opportunity to become the head coach of the rival Redskins, giving the Giants their first unofficial victory for the new season.

Following the Super Bowl victory parade up the Canyon of Heroes and a rally at Giants Stadium, Spagnuolo was whisked away on a private jet belonging to Washington owner Dan Snyder. It was clear Snyder wanted to make Spagnuolo an offer to succeed Joe Gibbs as head coach. But Spagnuolo called Snyder to tell him he'd be staying with the Giants, who in an aggressive and rare (for them) move ripped up Spagnuolo's contract and made him the NFL's highest-paid defensive coordinator. Gregg Williams made $1.9 million with the Redskins and will make that in his new job with the Jaguars.

"I appreciated Mr. Snyder giving me the opportunity to visit with him," Spagnuolo said. "I was happy to have the opportunity to explore that situation, but I am equally happy to be staying in New York and look forward to continued success with the Giants."

After his defense pounded Tom Brady for four quarters, perhaps no coach was more popular with Giants fans than Steve Spagnuolo.

This was a huge score for Spagnuolo, whose salary was in the $600,000 range, slightly above the average for defensive coordinators. The Giants as a rule do not go overboard on their assistant coaches, but they made it clear they would up the ante to keep Spagnuolo. His new deal pales in comparison to the $3 million per year Snyder would have paid for a head coach.

"This is unprecedented, their act of good will was extraordinary and it was immediate," Bob LaMonte, Spagnuolo's agent, told the *Post*. LaMonte said there was no discussion of promising Spagnuolo the Giants' head coaching job whenever Tom Coughlin retires.

"We have made the appropriate adjustments in our commitment to Steve in recognition of what he and the defensive coaches and players achieved this season," owner John Mara said.

Technically, Spagnuolo, 48, was not offered the Redskins job, but he would have been had he not preemptively said no thanks. LaMonte said Spagnuolo had a "wonderful meeting" with Snyder but that ultimately "his heart was in New York City."

No doubt, LaMonte also provided some historical perspective. He represented Mike Holmgren when, as an assistant coming off a Super Bowl victory with the 49ers, he turned down head coaching jobs with the Jets and Cardinals.

"Sometimes if you really analyze it, it's the job you turn down that propels you more than the job you take," LaMonte said. LaMonte also represented Marty Mornhinweg, a hot offensive assistant with the 49ers and Packers, who was hired as head coach of the Lions and lasted just two seasons.

"He went to a place where he was just decimated, and so was everyone else who went there," LaMonte said. "You don't want to go to a grave."

Having been spurned by Spagnuolo, Snyder instead promoted Jim Zorn to the top spot. The Seahawks quarterback had recently been hired as Washington's offensive coordinator after serving seven seasons as Seattle's quarterbacks coach.

"[Spagnuolo] really cares about his players more than I can tell you," LaMonte said. "It takes a real big guy with a lot of confidence to believe he can stay where he is and, I don't want to use the words *turn down*, have available to him an opportunity to interview for a job and then stay where he is. It seems to me this will have to be a feel-good story."

It sure feels good to the Super Bowl champion Giants. ▪

Spagnuolo is now the highest paid assistant coach in the game, making $2 million per season.

By Mike Puma

Players Ecstatic Spagnuolo Is Staying

The season is finished, but the Giants just picked up another win. At least that's how Giants linebacker Antonio Pierce and cornerback Aaron Ross reacted to the news that defensive coordinator Steve Spagnuolo is staying with the team. Spagnuolo withdrew his name from consideration for the Redskins head coaching vacancy and has a new three-year deal with the Giants that will make him the league's highest-paid defensive coordinator at $2 million per year.

"I'm glad the Giants' front office decided to keep the continuity of the team," Pierce said. "You win the Super Bowl, everybody is going to pick away from your team, and you don't want [Spagnuolo] going to a divisional rival, so that works out the best for us."

Though it's possible Redskins owner Dan Snyder wasn't going to offer Spagnuolo the job, perception is everything, and by announcing he's returning, Spagnuolo stands to increase his credibility within the organization.

"It just shows [Spagnuolo] is a real loyal person, first of all, by coming back to this team, when he could have easily been a head coach elsewhere," Ross said. "That speaks tremendously about him and makes you want to play for him even more. By making this move he got more respect from the defensive unit."

It was Spagnuolo's defensive unit that pounded Tom Brady in Super Bowl XLII on Sunday, allowing the Giants to rally for a 17–14 upset. Ross said it was the same defensive strategy the Giants employed in the regular-season finale, when the Patriots won 38–35.

"It was the same exact game plan: Go after Brady," Ross said. "Like we do every week, just blitz the quarterback, put pressure on the quarterback, and hope everything works out in our favor. We executed this game. Last game [against New England], we had some mental busts in the secondary, there were two big plays that we gave up, and it showed. [Spagnuolo] put us in a position to make plays. We really didn't have to do anything but study the film and execute his defense, and that made our job a lot easier."

Pierce was asked if he'd like to see Spagnuolo become a head coach. "Yeah, when I retire," he said. ■

Giants players were head over heels when they heard about Spags' decision to stay in New York.

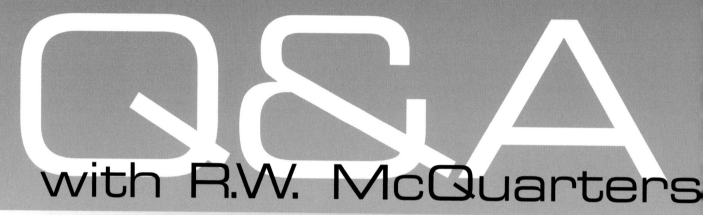

Q&A
with R.W. McQuarters

The *Post*'s Steve Serby chatted with the veteran Giants cornerback after he sealed the NFC divisional playoff victory over the Cowboys with an interception of Tony Romo.

Q: What has this week been like for you after your end-zone interception in Dallas?

A: Crazy.

Q: They introduced you at a Knicks game. Feel like a celebrity?

A: A little bit. This is New York, so it's gonna be amplified.

Q: They call you the Closer now.

A: The Finisher, the Closer…I like that.

Q: The flight home from Dallas?

A: It felt like we upset the world, and I felt like I had something to do with it. It really just made me feel good.

Q: Stephon Marbury is out for the year. Could you step in at point guard for the Knicks?

A: Yes, sir. I wish Mr. Thomas would give me a call.

Q: Why don't you call him?

A: Gotta wait till the off-season.

Q: What kind of a point guard are you?

A: More of a scorer-type. Like an [Allen] Iverson.

Q: Do you think you could have played in the NBA?

A: Yes.

Q: Why didn't you pursue basketball?

A: Because basketball really didn't pursue me. I didn't get invited to the Nike or ABCD camps out of high school because everybody assumed I was gonna play football.

A versatile athlete, R.W. McQuarters played Division I basketball and feels he could have made it to the NBA had he not focused on football.

After a long career in the NFL, journeyman McQuarters was finally able to reach the promised land and celebrate a world championship.

Q: Is basketball your first love?

A: Boxing was my first sport before I did anything [fourth grade]. My mother got me out of it because she knew what the sport did, just watching Muhammad Ali and others.

Q: You played basketball for Eddie Sutton for two years at Oklahoma State.

A: "It's a cardinal sin to shoot a jumper with your foot on the [three-point] line." He always said that. His thing was common-sense basketball, like why shoot a jumper with your foot on the line, when you can either get one step closer and it's a high-percentage shot, or take one step back and it's a three-pointer?

Q: Your oldest child, Robert William McQuarters III [10]?

A: Trey's a book guy, a school guy. He wants to be a quarterback.

Q: Rylan Winter [8]?

A: More of a daddy's little boy. Anything I'm doing, or anywhere I'm going, he wants to go. He's all football…wants to know how come I don't bring my helmet, my shoulder pads home. He always wants to come in the locker room. He wants my wristbands, my towels, gloves…he'll take my shoes. He knows they can't fit 'im, but he still wants 'em.

Q: Your daughter Reagan Winston [3]?

A: The most beautiful girl I've ever seen. Definitely a daddy's girl, like she doesn't like for me to leave her side at all.

Q: You've never been married. Describe an ideal mate.

A: I can tell you one thing that sums it all up—she needs to take care of me. Period.

Q: Deserted island, one woman?

A: The mother of my children.

Q: The first time you played against Brett Favre?

A: I was a rookie in San Francisco. Only thing I can remember is Brett Favre being Brett Favre…just gunning it.

Q: Ever intercept him?

A: Nope.

Q: The SpongeBob bandage you used to wear under your right eye?

A: Last year was Dora, SpongeBob, and a little bit of Scooby-Doo. So this year, it was Hello Kitty, but I ran out of Hello Kitty Band-Aids, so in my bag I just had a bunch of Band-Aids from last year, and I pulled out one, and it happened to be SpongeBob.

Q: Why under the right eye?

A: Demond Parker, we went to the same high school, and our first varsity game he said, "Man, we're gonna wear a Band-Aid up under the right eye." I don't know what it meant.

Q: Why did you originally grow dreadlocks as a rookie?

A: The movie *Metro*, Eddie Murphy was in it. And he had these little twisties. Then I got to a point I said, "I'm just gonna go ahead and lock it up." I let 'em lock, and I let 'em grow.

Q: Why did you cut them last March 21?

A: I turned 30 [the previous December]. It was time for a change. I let my children cut them.

Q: Your first reaction when you looked in the mirror?

A: I looked like my daddy (laughs).

Q: What happened when your teammates saw you at minicamp?

A: Some of 'em didn't even recognize me. They walked by me. And then personnel thought I was a new rookie that was just signed, so they walked right by me.

Q: Superstitions?

A: The Band-Aid. And I always say a prayer before I go out for pregame in the shower. With every punt return, I tighten up my gloves, but what I do is I pull it four times on each hand, and that's for my children and mother of my children. And then I give one big push [on the gloves] for both hands, and that's for family, that's together, for family. Then I straighten up my facemask. I kiss my daughter on the forehead by kissing my two fingers, and then I put it on the forehead.

Q: What's so much fun about punt returns?

A: Just me having the ball in my hands.

Q: Favorite childhood memory?

A: Getting a new bike for Christmas. It was like an SX 211.

Q: Boyhood idol?

A: Michael Jordan.

Q: Favorite movie?

A: *Gladiator.*

Q: Favorite actor?

A: Denzel.

Q: Favorite actress?

A: Halle Berry.

Q: Favorite entertainer?

A: Jay-Z.

Q: Favorite golf course?

A: Shadow Creek in Vegas.

Q: What's your handicap?

A: 20.

Q: Favorite meal?

A: Good ol' nice, home-cooked cheeseburger; well-done, with a bag of chips and some Kool-Aid.

Q: Best hamburger in New York?

A: I've never eaten a cheeseburger in the city of New York. You know why? 'Cause I eat a lot of steaks in New York! (Big smile). DelFrisco's, Ruth's Chris, Tao...Tao, ohmigod. They call it a kobe ribeye.

By George Willis

Reese Sees Title as Only the Beginning

Preparation for the 2008 season officially began less than a week after their Super Bowl XLII victory when Giants GM Jerry Reese assembled his staff of scouts and coaches to discuss the 2008 NFL draft. As they ate their first breakfast together as champions, Reese was already making plans to build an even stronger team to defend the franchise's latest Vince Lombardi Trophy.

"If you win the Super Bowl you might have a tendency to get complacent. We don't want to do that," Reese said at the team hotel about 12 hours after the Giants authored one of the biggest upsets in Super Bowl history over the Patriots at University of Phoenix Stadium.

"We're going to continue to beat the bushes and find the players to create competition. That's the key, to create competition going into training camp and make guys work and earn jobs."

The Giants certainly will savor their journey to excellence in Arizona, winning 11 straight road games, including four in the playoffs, and upsetting the previously unbeaten Patriots to win the franchise's third Super Bowl title. The victory parade was sweet, and the off-season brought endless accolades.

But the Giants should view this Super Bowl title as the beginning of something great and not the end. They are a young team that matured in the postseason, realizing their potential with a rugged, confident swagger that should only grow now that they have a shiny piece of jewelry to validate their talent. New England used its surprise Super Bowl victory in 2001 to build itself into the latest NFL dynasty. It's a blueprint Reese wants to follow.

"We just don't want to go away," Reese said. "So many times you see teams in the Super Bowl go away. New England set the bar high. For the last seven or eight years they've been on top. We'd like to get on a roll like that."

Physically, the talent is there, and youth

Jerry Reese and his staff want to see the Giants stay at the top of the NFL for many years.

said center Shaun O'Hara. "We kind of thrived in that situation. Now obviously the challenge next year is that everybody is going to be gunning for the Super Bowl winner. So that makes it even harder."

Reese has already stabilized the coach staff. Tom Coughlin was given a contract extension, while defensive coordinator Steve Spagnuolo turned down the Redskins head coaching position; and certainly there will be subtle changes in personnel. What won't change is the memory of the 2007 Giants. They have joined the '86 and '90 Giants in Super Bowl immortality and have earned the never-ending love of their fans like Super Bowl winners Harry Carson, Phil Simms, Lawrence Taylor, Ottis Anderson, and Carl Banks have enjoyed.

abounds. Quarterback Eli Manning is just coming of age. Players like Aaron Ross, Steve Smith, David Diehl, Corey Webster, Justin Tuck, Brandon Jacobs, and Ahmad Bradshaw are coming into their own. It's the Giants' mental approach that will be challenged. All year, they've thrived on being the underdog. They closed ranks after a 0–2 start and have taken pride in proving doubters wrong. Now they've exchanged labels from underdog to champion.

"One of the best things that happened to us this year was nobody expected much from us,"

"To be remembered and have this as part of our history is an unbelievable thing," Diehl said. "You see those guys and how proud they are to be New York Giants and part of this organization. Now 10 or 20 years down the road the bond that we've had all this season to win the championship, that bond will never change. We'll always be champions."

And maybe a dynasty in the making. ■

(above) While the championship is a great accomplishment, Reese hopes to see the Giants move into dynastic territory. (opposite) Reese has secured the coaching staff for several years, signing key members to extensions in the offseason.

Q&A
with Aaron Ross

The *Post's* Steve Serby chatted with the Giants' first-round pick from the University of Texas who had two interceptions in an October 2007 victory over the Jets.

Q: Describe the transformation that you undergo when you take the field.

A: I feel like I'm the most polite type of dude off the field, but when it comes to game time, I'm more vocal…it just brings the animal out of you.

Q: In what way?

A: I think most people, if they know me off the field, they wouldn't think I would just come and try to knock somebody's head off. I get more aggressive…more everything (chuckles).

Q: What was it like covering T.O. in the opener?

A: I'm used to keying someone's hips and this area (below the chest). The first time I lined up [against] him, I caught myself looking at his ankles, looking at his arms, looking at everything until the game sorta calmed down [for] me.

Q: What makes Vince Young such a great leader?

A: He puts everything on the line. You want to play for somebody like that.

Q: One Vince Young story from your UT days?

A: The summer before we won a national championship, he wrote on the board, "If you want to win the national championship, meet me at the bubble at 7:00 PM on Tuesdays and Thursdays." After workouts, we'd go do seven-on-seven and 11-on-11, so you could tell he was really focused on winning that national championship.

Q: Tell me about your mom.

A: She's a strong woman. My father left us when I was around 6 or 7; then my stepdad came into our [lives], not until I was like 12. She had me when she was 18, so me, her, and my brother are

Normally reserved off the field, Aaron Ross becomes an animal once he straps on his helmet.

A champion at both the collegiate and professional levels, Ross always finds the time to sign for fans.

really close…she's like my big sister. I didn't know we didn't have that much 'cause she would always provide and make sure we had what all the other kids had.

Q: Your father showed up on draft day at your mom's house in San Antonio?

A: I invited my grandmother—his mother—and he came.

Q: Since you were drafted, he's called you?

A: Yeah, he's been trying to get my grandmother to get in contact with me, but…

Q: It's not going to work?

A: Nah.

Q: So you don't forgive him for what he did?

A: I forgive him but, I mean, forgive and move on.

Q: Your girlfriend, 4x400m gold medalist Sanya Richards?

A: My mom ran track when she was in high school, so I took her to a big event called Texas Relays in Austin the summer before I went to UT. I didn't know who Sanya was, but I saw how she looked, so I was like, "I'm gonna get her when I get up here." I walked into the little dining hall, and she called me over, so I sorta played like I didn't know who she was (chuckles). She's brains and beauty.

Q: How did you celebrate your October 7 anniversary?

A: We just picked up some Burger King and went to the house and watched movies (chuckles).

Q: Sanya is living with you now; is she as good a cook as your mom?

A: I'm not answering that (chuckles)…well let me say this: my mom's better making American food, and she's better making Jamaican food.

Q: You write poems?

A: I really don't talk that much, so I really don't express my feelings. I have a lot to say, but I don't say it (chuckles).

Q: One line from a poem you wrote to Sanya?

A: I think it started out, "It was October 7, the day the Lord dropped you from heaven."

Q: You waited two years to go to UT because of a transcript issue…what odd jobs did you work?

A: I was a file clerk ($10 an hour) at a doctor's office, Dr. Tony, and a car detailer…washed cars ($9 an hour).

Q: Superstitions?

A: I call four people before the game and have them pray for me, since college: my mom and my stepdad, my pastor (Pastor Clark), and my girl.

Q: Hobbies?

A: Bowling. Once I buy a ball and get my spin down, I'll be good (chuckles).

Q: How do you feel about meetings starting five minutes early?

A: It was something I had to get used to; I was like, "What?" I was like, "It ain't time to go to meetings yet!" It's actually good 'cause now I have all my clocks set five minutes fast so I'm never late for anything.

Q: You liked basketball better until high school; who was your favorite player?

A: Allen Iverson.

Q: Boyhood idol?

A: My big brother (James); Deion Sanders.

Q: James is four years older?

A: He was faster, stronger, smarter, he was always just a step ahead of me in everything, so I was always striving to be what he was.

Q: Any chance you'll be another Prime Time?

A: I really hope I get to that level.

Q: Why do you enjoy big games?

A: Coming from the University of Texas (laughs)? That's what it is. And I don't shy away from competition. As a younger kid, I was always hanging with my big brother, so I was always competing with the best.

Q: Three dinner guests?

A: Martin Luther King, Jesus, my [childhood] pastor (the late J.D. Hamilton).

Q: Why your pastor?

A: He's the one that really grounded me when I was younger to know right from wrong, know about the Bible.

Q: What things would you do?

A: Not anything bad, but I'd get on a roof and jump off...things like that (chuckles).

Q: He saw you do it?

A: We had a playground, it was called the Yard; that's where all the kids that went to that church, he built that for us. He kept his eye on us. Right after school, I'd go to the Yard.

Q: And play what?

A: Kickball, jump rope, whatever you want to play, it was there (chuckles).

Q: Favorite New York things?

A: The shopping is great here, you can find anything you want (smiles).

Q: Favorite movie?

A: Anything with Martin Lawrence in it.

Q: Favorite actress?

A: Jada Pinkett.

Q: Favorite rapper?

A: Lil Wayne.

Q: Favorite meal?

A: Anything momma cooks...tacos.

By Mike Vaccaro

G-Men About Town After Super Bowl Win

They own the town again, and you would like to believe they will enjoy the ride every bit as much as their spiritual antecedents did. You would like to believe that this collection of Giants will permit New York to fall in love all over again, the way it did once, so hard that the feeling never went away, even across so many difficult autumns.

Once, the names were Gifford and Rote, Summerall and Huff, Robustelli and Modzelewski and Conerly and Tittle, and the names still roll off the tongue, because when they played, they not only played in New York, not only played for New York, they were of New York. They lived off the city's energy, fed off it, lent some of that star power back to the neon lights. They were Yankee Stadium on Sunday afternoons and Toots Shor on Friday night. They were everywhere: on billboards, on TV, in restaurants, in our conscience the way no team around here has ever been.

"We were like princes of the city," is the way Y.A. Tittle described it not long ago, the old quarterback's memory soaking in all those yellowing snapshots every bit the way an old fan's does. "In those days, the words *New York Giants* were pure magic. If you were on the team, you were set, and you were set up. Glorious days. Glorious."

Those Giants had their own forever run, too. It was 1956, the first year they had switched boroughs, left the crumbling Polo Grounds for Yankee Stadium across the Harlem River, and they had muddled their way to an 8–3–1 record, good enough for first place in the NFL's East Division, good enough to be served up as sacrificial lambs to the mighty Chicago Bears in the championship game. The Bears were heavily favored. But they ran into a buzz saw in the Bronx that day, got good and hammered 47–7, and the Giants legacy in New York was secured forever. Everything about the Giants was solidified in that year. The legendary waiting list for season tickets, one that now spans generations

In the city that invented the ticker tape parade, New Yorkers rise to recognize their championship heroes like Super Bowl MVP Eli Manning.

and includes wills and estates and occasional litigation settlements.

It all started with '56. Wellington Mara understood how important that team was; the rest of his life, the only piece of jewelry he ever wore was the championship ring that team earned him, and his son, John, wears that ring still.

"It was good that people were so excited about that championship," Gifford said a few years ago, "Because after that, we sure knew how to disappoint them."

On the field, maybe. On the field would come five more appearances in the championship game over the next seven seasons, and five losses: two to the Colts, two to the Packers, one to the Bears. There would be the '58 title game, which remains—all apologies to Giants 17, Patriots 14—the most important championship game ever played, the game that established pro football as America's secular religion. And after 1963, there would be 18 long years without a playoff appearance, a dry spell that's almost impossible to believe unless you're old enough to remember that endless pile of awful football.

"A lot of long Sundays," is how John Mara describes that time, "And a lot of sad Mondays." And even through all of that, they sold every ticket in the joint, even in those years when it seemed the Giants were an itinerant franchise, bouncing from Yankee Stadium to the Yale Bowl to Shea Stadium and then across the Hudson, to the Meadowlands, where they have stuffed close to 80,000 people in there every Sunday for 33 years, to the new place they will share with the Jets, the one across the parking lot, where the waiting list will continue to grow and grow.

"I grew up a Giants fan. There was a Giants fan in me when I coached there, and there's a Giants fan in me to this day," Bill Parcells said in 2006, while he was still coach of the detested Dallas Cowboys, recalling his youth in Oradell, N.J. "This is a team that gets in you when you're a kid and never lets go."

It was Parcells who led the great Giants renaissance of the 1980s, the team finally emerging from its hibernation to win its first two Super Bowls, a fresh batch of stars named Simms and Taylor and Carson and Bavaro adding to the team's legacy. Yet as good as that team was, it seemed almost to relish its place as a commuter franchise. The guts of the team, the offensive line, was called "The Suburbanites." They didn't shun the city, but they were very much Jersey's Team.

These Giants, these new champions, they embrace the city. They spend time in the city.

They love being announced at Knicks games, where they provide a presence of legitimacy in an otherwise rag-tag building. They eat here. They party here. They aren't afraid to land the occasional appearance on Page Six. And they drew a hearty gathering to the Canyon of Heroes, a rite the Parcells Giants never did enjoy.

"We're New Yorkers," said Plaxico Burress, in the aftermath of Super Sunday, "and that means something to us." It should. They own the town again. In a city that can be so obsessed with baseball, its heart once again belongs to a football team. You had better believe they will enjoy the ride. ■

Fans lined the parade route and the buildings above just hoping to snap a picture of their favorite Giants.

With Strahan's retirement, Umenyiora will have to be the Giants' leading quarterback cruncher.

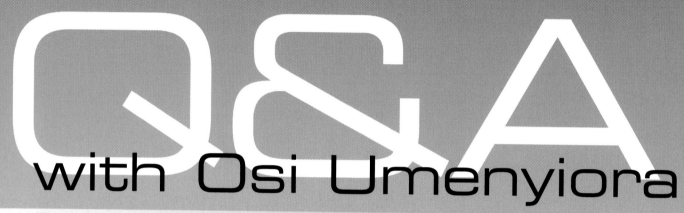

Q&A
with Osi Umenyiora

The *Post's* Steve Serby chatted with the Pro Bowl defensive end late in the 2007 season.

Q: What's better, sex or sacks?

A: Sacks. If I could go into a season knowing that if I didn't have sex the whole year, I'd get 20 sacks, I'd give up sex the whole year, every time.

Q: What's so great about sacks?

A: Just the feeling, man. There's nothin' like it. They're so hard to get, and you can go weeks and not get there. So when you finally do, it's just a different feeling.

Q: Who's your favorite quarterback to sack?

A: Obviously [Donovan] McNabb (six sacks earlier this season).

Q: Are you going to break Michael Strahan's Giants' sack record (141½)?

A: I don't know if I'm gonna be able to play that long. I'm at like 41 (40½). I might be able to get that.

Q: Another 10 years, 12 sacks a year...?

A: That would be like 160-something. I might be able to get that...nah...I don't think I'm gonna be able to play that long. I'm gonna put up numbers, though. As long as I'm healthy, I'm gonna put up numbers.

Q: Have you always been this confident?

A: Always! If you don't believe in yourself, who's gonna believe in you?

Q: Do you watch other pass rushers?

A: All the time. I like watching [Aaron] Schobel, Jason Taylor...I like watching myself, also.

Q: Why?

A: I constantly monitor myself, man. I have to see if my speed is up to par, if I'm getting off the line right, if my moves are crisp. I feel like I'm one of the best defensive ends in the league.

Umenyiora and the rest of the Giants defense were in Tom Brady's face all day during Super Bowl XLII.

Stopping the number one offense in the NFL in their tracks, the Giants forced the Patriots into uncharacteristic mistakes.

Q: Do you notice fear in quarterbacks' eyes?

A: No, but in the offensive tackles, I see it in their face. You can tell when they're nervous, or you can look 'em in the eye and they'll look away. The ones who look back at you (chuckles), you know you're gonna have a long day.

Q: Who are those?

A: [Chris] Samuels, Tra Thomas, Flozell Adams. Those guys look right back at you.

Q: What are you like before kickoff?

A: Super quiet. I'll be going over what I have to do over and over again.

Q: Describe the transformation.

A: You have to turn into a different person, man. These guys have families to feed.

Q: The best joke Tom Coughlin cracked this year?

A: He mispronounced a word one time, and that was pretty much the funniest thing he said. I forgot what the word was, though. Besides that, he hasn't really cracked any jokes.

Q: I thought he was a different guy this year.

A: Maybe practice is a little different. We haven't put on pads like since Week 2. Besides that, I don't think he's really changed much.

Q: You're on the Leadership Council. How has that been beneficial?

A: There's really no dissension. Everybody's on the same page.

Q: Why was there so much dissension last year?

A: We didn't really have input in anything even though we were the ones who were doing all the stuff he (Coughlin) was asking us to do. It was just his way, and that was it.

Q: Do you think Coughlin is definitely coming back?

A: I'm not really like a general manager, but I wish he comes back.

A very confident person, Umenyiora believes in himself and in his abilities.

Q: You do?

A: He's a great football coach, man.

Q: If you win today, who dumps the Gatorade bucket on Coughlin?

A: Me and Mike [Strahan] again. We did it in 2005 when we beat Oakland to go to the playoffs.

Q: Describe your ideal girl.

A: She'd have to be very womanly. And she has to be smart, 'cause I like to fancy myself an intelligent individual. We gotta be able to have a conversation. She has to be decent looking, but I'm not gonna say a knockout. She has to be an all-around good person, has to get along with my family and everybody who I surround myself with.

Q: Describe your personality.

A: Very gregarious. I'm pretty funny…likeable guy sometimes…sometimes you'd hate me, sometimes you'd like me. There's really no in-between.

Q: Why would somebody not like you?

A: 'Cause sometimes my supposed cockiness might rub you the wrong way even though most of the time I'm just joking. I play around a lot, and people might take that seriously. But if you actually know me, there's no way you wouldn't like me.

Q: What is Strahan like outside the workplace?

A: He gets wild. Not wild-wild, but you see him dancing, enjoying himself…he's fun to hang out with. Very boisterous.

Q: Something funny about Justin Tuck?

A: Justin Tuck has very, very short fingers.

Q: Give me a funny story about Barry Cofield.

A: Cofield's the most sarcastic person ever. Someone will tell a joke and everybody would laugh, and then he'll just give like the fakest laugh ever (chuckle).

Q: Fred Robbins?

A: Doesn't say much. I don't know any funny stories about him.

Q: How about as a player?

A: Very, very quick. We call him Fast Feet Freddie 'cause of how fast his feet move on the pass rush.

Q: What would you want your peers to say about you?

A: That my word is my bond. That's the one [characterestic] in people that I admire most. I just want them to say that…and I was a helluva football player.

Q: Favorite New York restaurant?

A: Phillipe's. After we make the playoffs, I'm gonna take you…my treat.

By Mike Vaccaro

Coughlin's Wins of Change

All week long, to the point of exhaustion, Tom Coughlin stood tall and he answered the same question posed in a thousand different ways. How did you change? Why did you change? Was it difficult to change? Do you have change for a five? At what point did you know you needed to change? David Bowie could have been his interpreter.

Turn and face the strange (ch-ch-changes)…

All week long, Coughlin hung in there like Eli Manning in the pocket, never once lost patience with the subject, even though he knew as well as everyone else milling about those various Super Bowl podiums the *real* questions lurking underneath.

"How did it feel to be told you had to change or lose your job? Were you really an ogre before? Are you comfortable with this kinder, gentler you? Do you still have to get to meetings 10 minutes early?"

On his first full day as a Super Bowl–winning coach—the title he will carry the rest of his life, the accomplishment that will be in the first sentence of his obituary—Coughlin finally revealed something else about the way he approached this season and the reasons why he altered that approach.

"It was time," he said, "to start having fun, and to enjoy this job."

And you know something? All coaches should enjoy such an epiphany, achieve such a moment of clarity. The big coaches, the successful ones, they spend so much time on the chase, pursuing players, and better jobs, and richer salaries, and higher levels of competition, that it's become anathema to admit just how cool it is to be one of the 32 men who work as NFL head coaches.

"I always evaluate who I am and what I can do to be better," Coughlin said. "And to me, it was critical to be able to maximize the things about this life that I enjoy the most."

Sure, Coughlin had to change in order to

Tom Coughlin changed his coaching approach slightly in 2007: he decided it was time to start enjoying himself and having fun.

AP Images

save his job, to keep a career that would never again have included another NFL job if he'd been fired from this one, at age 61. Yes, Coughlin needed to improve communication with his players, needed to invent that leadership council, needed to physically keep ajar the door to his office he'd always insisted was open.

"There were things we wanted to hear from Tom because, quite frankly, I wanted to make sure this was still an environment where he wanted to work," John Mara said earlier in the week. "It wasn't just a one-way street: 'Tom, do this or you're gone.' We valued him and didn't want him to be uncomfortable, either. Because it seemed like he was miserable at times last year."

Misery, of course, can be a coach's closest companion, if he lets it. The agony of losing always far surpasses the ecstasy of winning. You can be consumed in details, destroyed by misfortune. And if you happen to wear emotions on your expressive Irish face, the way Coughlin tends to, then the television cameras become an additional tormenter.

"There were times," a friend of Coughlin's confided yesterday, "when he would look at himself on TV and his shoulders would sag and he'd say, 'That's just terrible. That's not me. Why do I look that way?' And I'd tell him, 'That's how you always have looked your whole life. It's just that people notice it more when you coach the New York Giants.'"

See, that's the chapter of the story everyone failed to pick up all week. Those changes? They were mutually beneficial. The Giants got a coach they could communicate with, relate to, understand. And Coughlin retrieved that part of his soul that led him to this wildly bruising, itinerant life in the first place. It was a transfiguration that may have started early last January, when he convinced his bosses that he really was a player's coach at heart. And one that ended late Sunday night in the Giants' locker room at University of Phoenix Stadium with Antonio Pierce, one of the toughest nuts any coach has ever had to crack, wrapping Coughlin in a long embrace.

"Look at what you did," the coach said.

"Couldn't have done it without you," the linebacker said.

The job probably never seemed more fun, more enjoyable, than at that exact moment. ∎

The changes in Coughlin's style benefited everyone with the Giants and led to the ultimate prize: a championship.

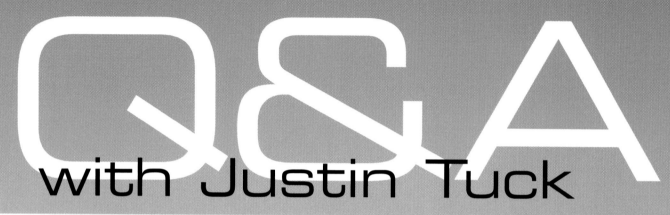

Q&A
with Justin Tuck

The *Post's* Steve Serby chatted with the defensive end from Notre Dame, who was second on the Giants with 10 sacks, prior to the 2008 divisional playoffs game against the Cowboys.

Q: [Tonight] around 7:30, what do you visualize?

A: Some camera catching a snapshot of me pushing off of [Tony] Romo on the ground with the ball in his hand with three zeroes on the clock…with the Giants winning.

Q: Terrell Owens grew up around the corner from you (in Kellyton, Alabama).

A: I knew of him; there were stories about him when he was in high school. It gets hot in the summers. He used to jog the town center in midday in a jogging suit and a book bag on his shoulders. He used to jog around with bricks in his book bag.

Q: You'd like Jessica Simpson at the game?

A: 'Cause I want to beat Tony Romo at his best; I think he'll play better with Jessica there…I'm joking.

Q: Can't she be a distraction?

A: I don't know; that depends on Romo. I think if she's a distraction, she can be a distraction if she's at the game or not at the game, so I don't really weigh in on that.

Q: Antonio Pierce's best trash-talking moment?

A: When he walks up to the line of scrimmage and the quarterback's making checks, [he'll say] "That's not gonna work," and bleep like that.

Q: Any one particular player he got into it with?

A: The Miami game, this O-lineman named [Rex] Hadnot; they got into it pretty good.

Q: What was he telling him?

A: He told him something about, "You're the reason

A smiling face when appearing out of uniform, Justin Tuck is feared by opposing quarterbacks once he takes the field.

With 10 sacks during the regular season, Tuck has quickly become one of the top defensive players in the game.

why they ain't winning. Your name is Hadnot." That was him and Osi [Umenyiora].

Q: How about you?

A: I don't talk, unless I'm provoked.

Q: What's the best speech Michael Strahan has given on the field just before kickoff?

A: I can't repeat it.

Q: Because it's X-rated?

A: Yes.

Q: You expect another this Sunday?

A: Absolutely.

Q: You guys like it?

A: Yeah…we're different people out on that football field.

Q: Different people how?

A: That's kinda like on a battleground, so we become kind of warriors, I guess, if that ain't too cliche.

Q: How do you describe that transformation?

A: I don't; I can't. It's kinda like people that drive NASCAR, they really say the rush that they get driving 200 miles per hour you really can't explain.

Q: You liked the Cowboys growing up?

A: I actually did, I'm embarrassed to say that, but I did.

Q: Quarterback you'd love to sack?

A: [Tom] Brady. I hit him a lot, but I didn't sack him. Hopefully, we get to sack him some this year.

Q: Your Lisfranc (foot) fracture 15 months ago in Texas Stadium?

A: It was me going against [Marc] Colombo, I think. [Drew] Bledsoe threw the ball real quick, so I planted to run to the football, and as soon as I planted, I guess, I twisted some way or another, and I guess it just popped there.

Q: How did growing up with five sisters toughen you up?

A: They used to jump on me. I was kinda annoying at times.

Q: What would you do to annoy them?

A: Messing up dishes that they had to wash sometimes. After they'd wash 'em, I'd come in right behind 'em and mess up a dish.

Q: Describe Kellyton.

A: Small…quiet…peaceful.

Q: Just like Manhattan?

A: Just like it, man. Manhattan probably has about 10 million more people…a few more traffic lights.

Q: How many traffic lights in Kellyton?

A: None. We have a caution light.

Q: What was there to do?

A: You stayed outside, you threw the football around, you played basketball from sunup to sundown…you cut grass.

Q: Did you make money cutting grass?

A: My whole street is only Tucks, and I was kinda

like the male stud of the family at the time, so I got the opportunity to cut everybody's yard on Saturday.

Q: Describe your father.

A: Mild temper; it takes a lot for him to really get upset. If he's ever upset, you know you've done something that you really didn't have no business doing.

Q: What's the most upset he's gotten at you?

A: Probably a report-card grade.

Q: Any particular subject?

A: Social studies. I just didn't like this teacher; I'm stubborn, so I just decided I wasn't gonna do any work.

Q: How old were you?

A: Seventh grade.

Q: Did your social studies grade improve after that?

A: It went up 72 points.

Q: How did you propose to your fiancée (Lauran Williamson) a year ago?

A: I got on my knee and asked her did she want to marry me.

Q: Where was it?

A: At her house [in Connecticut]. I'm not that big of a romantic. I'm kind of a to-the-point guy.

Q: Adalius Thomas is your older cousin.

A: His father and my father are first cousins. I've seen hits that he had on guys, it was just like,

"Wow! Do I want to play football?"

Q: You started out as tight end your first two weeks at Notre Dame before they switched you to defense.

A: I like hitting people; I didn't necessarily like getting hit.

Q: Boyhood idol?

A: He-Man.

Q: Favorite childhood memory?

A: First time I beat my brother [Raleigh] in a basketball game. I was 12 and he was 20.

Q: Hobbies?

A: I got a '70 Chevelle I'm working over now.

Q: Three dinner guests?

A: Martin Luther King, Jesus, Gandhi.

Q: Favorite movie?

A: *Braveheart; Gladiator.*

Q: Favorite actor?

A: Denzel Washington.

Q: Favorite actress?

A: Julia Roberts.

Q: Favorite entertainer?

A: Marvin Gaye.

Q: Favorite meal?

A: Fried chicken and collard greens.

By Bart Hubbuch

Accorsi Always Believed

Even in retirement, Ernie Accorsi couldn't avoid the kind of second-guessing that's made New York fans famous. Accorsi, the Giants' former general manager, was sitting with his children in a section of the team's rowdy fans during the final, heart-stopping moments of Super Bowl XLII. When Eli Manning, Accorsi's handpicked franchise passer, overthrew a wide-open Plaxico Burress during a critical Big Blue drive, a nearby fan wheeled around to Accorsi and screamed, "Your quarterback just cost us a chance at the world championship!"

When Manning followed that a few minutes later by throwing the game-winning touchdown to Burress in the Giants' epic 17–14 upset of the Patriots, that same fan had a much different reaction.

"He tried to kiss me on the lips!" Accorsi said. Accorsi retired after last season, handing the reins to Jerry Reese, but—thanks largely to the draft-day trade with the Chargers he made in 2004 to land Manning—he is still considered the primary architect of Sunday's Super Bowl victory.

Asked if the Lombardi Trophy not coming until after he stepped down was a bittersweet moment for him, Accorsi bristled. "No, it's not bittersweet," he said. "I don't know how there could be anything bitter about this." Accorsi said the tension during the Giants' final drive was almost overwhelming.

"I was with my kids, and we never watch a game together," he said. "I can't even explain it. I was numb. I felt really emotional during that whole drive because I didn't know if [Manning] was going to be able to do it. When we got the ball, I just said, 'If he is what we thought he was, he's got to do it now.'"

Manning came through, marching the Giants 83 yards in 12 plays for the epic score. But Accorsi said the touchdown didn't leave him feeling vindicated after absorbing so much criticism for the Chargers trade while Manning struggled.

"I have a thick skin," he said, "And it was too great of a moment to even think about that." ■

The primary architect of the Giants championship squad, Ernie Accorsi was responsible for the trade on draft day that made Eli Manning a Giant.

Although the trade was maligned by many Giants fans, Accorsi knew that one day Manning would pay big dividends.

By Paul Schwartz

Strahan Reaches End of the Road

The hangdog look on the face of Giants defensive end Osi Umenyiora was all anyone needed to see to confirm the surprising, but hardly shocking, news that Michael Strahan retired.

"I'm happy for him," Umenyiora said softly, "But I'm sad for myself."

As Strahan's closest buddy on the team, Umenyiora had spoken to Strahan enough during the past few months to know there was a chance the end was here. But he could not erase in his mind the recent memory of Strahan, as usual, menacing the opponent from his defensive end position, and the hope that he'd do it again as the Giants look to defend their Super Bowl title.

"The way he was playing, the way he was producing, I thought at least he'd give it another year or two," Umenyiora said. "I talked to him a couple of times, he was back and forth a little bit. He was tired of the game a little bit, but he was playing so well you kind of don't want to leave the game like that."

After 15 seasons with the Giants that will surely make him a first-ballot Hall of Famer in five years—assuming he stays retired—Strahan, at the age of 36, with an enormous Super Bowl ring now slipped on his finger, has bid adieu. He informed the team of his retirement plans, and word slowly filtered to coach Tom Coughlin, who was inside the bubble putting the Giants through their sixth and final Organized Team Activity practice. As the entire team prepared to gather for the start of a mandatory three-day mini-camp in June, Strahan was not part of the team for the first time since before the 1993 season.

"It was important that my teammates knew which way I was going before they get out on the field to start the work to defend our title," Strahan told Foxsports.com from California. "It's time. I'm done. It's a tough decision. But I wanted to be fair to the Giants and fair to my teammates."

Strahan's agent, Tony Agnone, told the *Post* this timing was not a coincidence.

After being a fixture on the Giants for 15 years, Michael Strahan finally decided to walk away.

"Mini-camp was his time," Agnone said. "He said if he's not motivated by then, he's not going to do it."

Co-owner John Mara got the news with a morning call from Strahan, who also alerted co-owner Steve Tisch and GM Jerry Reese and left a message for Coughlin.

"I told him I was disappointed and that I knew he could still play at a very high level, and we were hoping to have him back," Mara said. "But I certainly understand his decision. I told him he's been a great Giant. He thanked me for everything the organization has done for him. I told him 'I think you've done more for us than we can ever do for you.'"

Coughlin called his relationship with Strahan, "very close, very special" and added, "It was the perfect time for Michael to retire."

Life after Strahan will be quite different around the Giants, because for so long he was the best and most vocal player, an outsized personality capable of great wit and humor, at times followed almost immediately by harsh bombast. In his later years, he developed into more of a true team leader who never lost his love of the locker room or the camaraderie present within.

He never lost his touch as a player. Strahan had nine sacks last season, giving him a franchise record 141½ in his career, good for fifth on the NFL all-time list. For those adamant that Lawrence Taylor is the true Giants record-holder (Taylor's 9½ sacks as a rookie in 1981 don't count because sacks were not yet an official statistic), Strahan finished one-half sack shy of Taylor's total of 142.

Strahan's 22½ sacks in 2001 remain an NFL single-season record, and he was selected seven times to the Pro Bowl. His 216 regular-season games played for the Giants is a team record, but they took a toll, as Strahan often listed the beating his body took over the years as a prime reason for edging toward retirement.

Despite those constant reminders, the Giants, from the front office down to the players, expected him to return. He was due $4 million for this season (that now comes off the Giants' salary cap) and Agnone said the team came up with "a little more money for him" a while back.

Asked if he thinks Strahan will ever play again, Agnone said, "Oh, gosh, no. One thing we talked about was when you retire, buddy, you retire. Now, if the Giants are going to the Super Bowl and say 'Okay, Michael, let's rock and roll,' maybe. But I would say it would be highly unlikely."

Strahan, who resides in California, is expected to go directly into broadcasting while the Giants move on to try to defend their title.

"He will be missed," quarterback Eli Manning said. "He's a tremendous leader of this team, got a great attitude, great work ethic, he's taught a lot of young players coming in, to see how you're supposed to act as a football player." ■

A team leader both on and off the field, Strahan's presence will be missed by everyone in the Giants locker room.

"We knew we had to get to Tom Brady. If we
didn't do that, then we weren't going to win the game."
—Michael Strahan on the Giants' Super Bowl defensive mission

"When you're a Giant, you're a Giant for life; I feel that, I know that. That will absolutely never change. I'm looking forward to watching these guys, guys I'm going to always call my teammates, not ex-team-mates. I'm not an ex-Giant and they're not my ex-teammates."

—Michael Strahan at his retirement press conference at Giants Stadium

"This is a whole different story...New England was 18–0 and talking about history. We had heard a lot this time about how we had no shot, but we shocked the world."
—Michael Strahan on the Giants' Super Bowl win

By Paul Schwartz

2008 Preview: Does Magic Have an Encore?

We shall soon see what the Giants have in store for 2008 after leaving behind one of the most stunning, unexpected championship rides ever seen. Their 17–14 humbling of the previously unbeaten Patriots in Super Bowl XLII was the second-greatest upset in the history of the grand game, and the improbability of the triumph was reflected in the gratitude and incredulity of those touched by the celebration.

The confetti has long since been swept up from the Canyon of Heroes and the white-gold Tiffany-inspired rings have already been sized and slipped onto their fingers. Tom Coughlin, Eli Manning, David Tyree, Michael Strahan, Plaxico Burress, and so many others will always be saluted for bringing such glory and honor to one of the NFL's hallmark franchises. The cheering, though, has been resigned to a cherished memory, and the time has come to move on.

No longer an upstart team on a nice little surge, the Giants assuredly will not be favored as a repeat Super Bowl winner, but they wear the crown, and that changes everything.

"It's against the odds of doing it again," said Manning, who in a late-season six-week span blossomed into the savior the franchise envisioned him to be en route to an MVP-winning Super Bowl showing. "I still don't know how much respect this team has gotten. We made a great run through the playoffs, but no matter what game we won we were always the underdog in a big way in every game we played in the playoffs. I think we still have a lot left to prove. A lot of it is maybe just to ourselves, that we can become a better team. We got hot at the right time last year, but we can't afford to wait to the end to do it again. We need to become a better team full-time."

While it's convenient to consider 2007 an enchanted Giants season, in fact it was less fairy tale and far more the deserved reward for gutting

Eli Manning will be a big part of a Giants team that will be looking to re-create last season's magic and winning formula.

it out. The Giants were grit, not glitz. They were about fortitude, not merely good fortune. There was nothing new-wave about the defensive bludgeoning they inflicted on opponents or the manner in which Manning's offense developed into a mistake-free, high-efficiency operation. Coughlin as the head coach was no sudden genius, but a man of conviction who never shed his values while evolving into a leader his players could trust.

Even the signature moment that captivated hearts and confounded the Patriots was borne out of steady and determined effort. There's no hyperbole at work in labeling the Manning-to-Tyree 32-yard pass play in the closing minute of Super Bowl XLII the single-greatest moment in NFL championship history. Actually, it was two of the greatest moments—Manning's incredible escape and throw followed by Tyree's improbable leap, snatch, and catch while pinning the ball on the side of his helmet. Fate? Perhaps. But Manning's coolness under fire is a character trait he's cultivated, and Tyree's physical accomplishment was a credit to the perseverance he's displayed while repeatedly defying the odds as he waged an annual battle to carve a niche for himself on the roster.

It was impossible to view what the Giants created and completed and not feel moved, which is why in so many venues outside of the New England region this was such a popular victory. They lost their very first game of the season on the road in Dallas and then embarked on an unprecedented trip, winning all seven of their remaining road games in the regular season and then producing playoff upsets in sunny Tampa, hostile Dallas, and frigid Green Bay. The Giants were designated as the road team in Super Bowl XLII, as they won their record 11th consecutive game away from home. Even the vanquished acknowledged the Giants as a team with remarkable qualities.

"I have a lot of respect for that team, because they work hard and they have a lot of great leaders," said Patriots quarterback Tom Brady, who was denied a fourth Super Bowl ring as he tried and failed to withstand a furious defensive Giants assault. "It's kind of a blue-collar team. When you lose a game you at least want to lose to guys you respect. And I certainly respect those guys."

This was undeniably an "innocent climb," the phrase coined by Pat Riley to describe a season where the wonderment of winning is new and shiny, where pressure is low and skeptics are many. Slightly after midseason the Giants basically conceded the NFC East crown to the Cowboys, and late-season Giants Stadium losses to the Vikings and Redskins made any real playoff run an unlikely scenario. The Giants staggered to a playoff-clinching victory in snowy Buffalo and then refused to back down from the unbeaten Patriots in a regular-season-ending shootout loss. That was the spark that ignited Manning and sent the Giants on their way, but a new year brings new standards of excellence to measure up to.

For Manning and the rest of the Giants, 2008 brings new challenges and new opportunities.

"Everybody understands the history of Super Bowl participants," center Shaun O'Hara said. "The statistics are against you to make it back to the playoffs. We all understand the work that's ahead of us. One of the toughest things in the NFL to handle is success. I think we've shown we're no different."

Recreating the esprit de corps born out of an underdog mentality is a great challenge awaiting the Giants, as success and money and fame and glory have a way of blunting the willingness of individuals to sacrifice in the name of the team.

"You got to come out of the clouds," Tyree said. "It's a euphoria that comes along with winning the championship. You got to come out of the clouds, come out of the euphoria."

The Giants believe they have the perfect coach to snap to attention a team and ground it in reality. Coughlin at the age of 61 loosened the firm and often unyielding grasp he stubbornly clenched like a fist and finally reached the mountaintop, and no one looked and sounded more proud of the results. But he is immune to distractions—even after he was rewarded with a three-year extension that binds him contractually to the Giants through the 2011 season—and there is absolutely no fear of satisfaction ever creeping into Coughlin's psyche.

"There is always a sense of complacency when you win the Super Bowl, all the way across the board, from the top to the very bottom," said general manager Jerry Reese, who in his first year calling the shots inherited some quality from Ernie Accorsi and augmented the talent base to create a championship team. "You have to fight against that. I think our head coach won't let that happen. I think we are still hungry."

There's no doubt the Giants captivated the imaginations of so many NFL fans, and thus it is no surprise that as Super Bowl champs they will kick off the 2008 season with the featured Thursday night season debut, coming September 4 against the NFC East rival Redskins at Giants Stadium. There are at least three more prime-time night games for the Giants, who will need to prove that their uncanny Road Warrior success was no fluke with tough (and rare, for them) visits to Cleveland and Pittsburgh. There's also a cross-country trek to Arizona to face the Cardinals. Of course, the Giants won't mind at all returning to Glendale, Arizona, and University of Phoenix Stadium, the site of their incredible upset of the Patriots that some have dubbed the Miracle in the Desert.

There's unquestionably a chance for a fast start, as following the Redskins in the opener the Giants face the Rams in St. Louis and return home to play the Bengals prior to an earlier-than-appreciated bye in Week 4. Figure the November 2 midseason division battle with the Cowboys at Giants Stadium will be filled with intrigue, considering it was the Giants who unceremoniously bounced the 'Boys from last season's playoffs by subduing Tony Romo and

Kevin Boss is one of the young players the Giants will look to more frequently in 2008 after his emergence in last year's playoffs.

turning girl-pal Jessica Simpson into a fair-haired symbol of doom in Dallas.

As always, the 2008 version of the Giants will not be an identical match to the champions that came before them, but much of the roster returns intact. There's the pulverizing pass rush now led by Osi Umenyiora and Justin Tuck; the brains of the operation in middle linebacker Antonio Pierce and young cornerbacks Aaron Ross and Corey Webster. New on the scene is a rookie safety, Kenny Phillips, who should immediately see the field, and a veteran safety, Sammy Knight, who has made a career of delivering jarring tackles.

Manning is obviously entrenched as the marquee quarterback, and his sensational postseason performances reserved a forever place for him in New York sports lore. His weapons are plentiful, from Plaxico Burress, Amani Toomer, Steve Smith, and David Tyree at receiver, to Jeremy Shockey and Kevin Boss at tight end, to the thunder of Brandon Jacobs and lightning of Ahmad Bradshaw at running back.

Punter and level-headed Jeff Feagles is back for his 21st NFL season and also returning to the scene is Lawrence Tynes, who kicked the Giants into the Super Bowl when he booted a frozen football 47 yards in arctic Lambeau Field in the NFC title game. Coughlin's staff remains intact, with prize defensive coordinator Steve Spagnuolo resisting head-coaching inquiries elsewhere to continue his defensive dominance with the Giants.

Reese struck gold last year as his first draft class as general manager imported seven players who made real contributions as rookies. Reese is hoping for more of the same with his 2008 crop that includes Phillips, cornerback Terrell Thomas (USC), and receiver Mario Manningham (Michigan).

"That's what we're working for," Reese said. "We'd like to stay at a high level. The bar's been set pretty high for us, and we want to stay up there. We want to have some stability and stay at a high level. The league's not built like that. It's built for any team to be able to come out of nowhere and win a Super Bowl. That's the beauty of the National Football League. Everybody has a chance when you can stay on top—I kind of marvel how New England has been able to stay on top—and we'd like to stay at a high level as well."

The Giants of 2007 reached the highest level possible but should be able to settle back down to earth soon enough.

"Heck," O'Hara said, "everybody's picking the Cowboys to win the division, right?" ■

Manning will have some great targets to throw to, including big play rookie Mario Manningham.

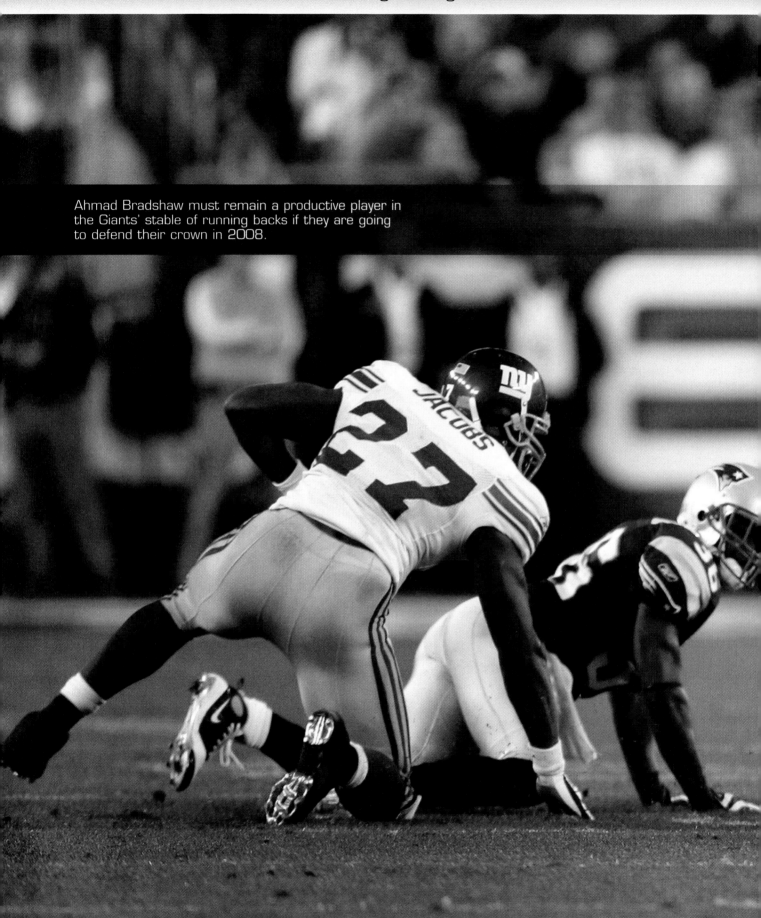

Ahmad Bradshaw must remain a productive player in the Giants' stable of running backs if they are going to defend their crown in 2008.

With Brandon Jacobs battering teams on the ground and Manning beating them through the air, the Giants should remain a potent and balanced offense in 2008.